CREATIVITY IN CONTEXT

How to make a poet

**Monica Carroll
& Jen Webb**

PRAGMATICS OF ART

University of Canberra

Centre for Creative and Cultural Research

Series editor: Distinguished Professor Jen Webb

1. Pierre Bourdieu, *Thinking about Art – at Art School* Translated by Michael Grenfell. Edited by Scott Brook.
2. Ronald Schleifer, *Practical Reasoning: How the experience of the Humanities can help train doctors*. Edited with an introduction by Jen Crawford.
3. Monica Carroll & Jen Webb, *Creativity in context: How to make a poet.*

CREATIVITY IN CONTEXT

How to make a poet

**Monica Carroll
& Jen Webb**

PRAGMATICS OF ART 3

University of Canberra
Centre for Creative and Cultural Research

First published in 2018 by
Centre for Creative and Cultural Research, with Recent Work Press
Faculty of Arts and Design, University of Canberra, ACT 2601
Australia

This publication is copyright. Apart from any fair dealing for the
purpose of private study, research, criticism or review, as permitted
under the Copyright Act 1968, no part may be reproduced by
any process without written permission. Enquiries should be made
to the publisher.

© Authors: Monica Carroll, Jen Webb
© the publisher, for the publication concept, layout and design

ISBN: ISBN 978-0-64840-420-0 (paperback)

Series editor: Jen Webb
Publication editor: Shane Strange
Publication design and layout: Caren Florance

Cover image: 'Water Ballet' by Mary (goodsardine):
https://flic.kr/p/5bbJEz

Contents

- vi   Series introduction:
- 1   Introduction
- 5   The project: Understanding creative excellence: A case study in poetry
  - *9   Table 1: The poets in the project (n=76)*
- 10   Characteristics of highly successful poets
  - *10   Table 2: Age range for poets in the study (n=76)*
  - *12   Table 3: Attachments, by category of poet (n=66)*
  - *13   Table 4: Education levels attained (%)*
  - *15   Table 5: Status of poets by gender (%)*
- 16   From child to poet: The role of memory
  - *19   Table 6: Stage of schooling where poetry was first encountered (%) (n=67)*
  - *21   Table 7: Reported age of first encounter. Comparing age at first encounter between categories of poet (%) (n=67)*
  - *24   Table 8: Reported experience of first encounter prior to tertiary education (%) (n=67)*
  - *25   Table 9: The matchmaker*
  - *26   Table 10: The role of the matchmaker, by group of poets*
  - *28   Table 11: Type of influence of significant person*
  - *29   Table 12: Type of influence of significant person, by category*

- 32 Teachers of influence: Switching on the poet
  - *33 Table 13: What happened in the classroom?*
- 37 Myth of the lone poet
  - *47 Table 14: Gender and community attachments*
- 48 The state of poetry
- 55 Conclusion
- 56 Acknowledgements
- 57 Sources

Series Introduction

The Centre for Creative and Cultural Research (CCCR) within the Faculty of Arts and Design at the University of Canberra focuses on applied research into creative practice. Staff, research students, adjuncts and visitors work on key challenges within the creative field and the cultural sector. The focus of our work is to conduct imaginative and practical experiments at the intersection of creative writing, digital technology and contemporary heritage practice. Many of the CCCR's members are creative practitioners who produce not only traditional scholarly outputs, but also creative publications and performances, exhibitions and exhibition design, and professional inputs to cultural and community institutions. Poetry, material poetics, narrative practices and exhibition practices are at the heart of our research activity. In addition, the CCCR facilitates a series of intensive creative workshops with people suffering from trauma and related issues, and is developing knowledge and skills about the relationship between art practice, creative thinking, and resilience.

This series, The Pragmatics of Art, aims to model and disseminate the combination of practical and intellectual research that guides the work of our Centre, and to provide thoughtful contributions from a wide variety of sources to artistic and intellectual projects that both derive from and serve larger communities. In a way, the series represents a working laboratory for students, artists, and scholars interested in learning to integrate the arts and skills of artistic knowledges and design into other branches of practical and intellectual work in our society.

>Distinguished Professor Jen Webb
>
>*Director,*
>*Centre for Creative and Cultural Research*
>*University of Canberra*
>
>*General Editor,*
>*The Pragmatics of Art*

Introduction

In the late 2000s Kevin Brophy, Jen Webb and Paul Magee – all of us both poets and university-based scholars – began talking seriously about investigating links between poetry, knowledge and creativity. For well over a decade we had observed, and been intimately involved in, the growing number of creative writers enrolling in doctoral degrees. Many of these doctoral students, rather than following the conventional path of literary analysis, chose to use the processes and movements of their own creative writing to build knowledge about their research question. This approach may seem *de rigueur* now, after twenty plus years of creative doctorates being conducted and completed by artists across Australian universities, but ten or fifteen years ago it was a different landscape. Much explanation was needed to justify this mode of research. Even more justification was required to explain why taxpayer-funded doctorates should be pursued in a creative mode.

All three of us had also, for a decade and more, been writing poetry, reading poetry and exploring the scholarly and technical literature on poetry; reading what poets said about their own work and its motivating factors; and thinking about how poetry makes – if not the world, at least fractions of that world – go round. And we had researched and published extensively on related issues: Kevin

Brophy focusing on creativity, Paul Magee on creative practice, and Jen Webb on creative research. Building on this background and on our shared interests, we completed a pilot project on the question of poetry and knowledge, and then began the process of applying for funding for a more substantial project. At this point the University of Hertfordshire's Professor Michael Biggs – a leading international figure in the field of arts research – joined the team. Together we structured the project 'Understanding Creative Excellence: a case study in poetry', and gratefully accepted funding from the Australian Research Council (ARC). Joining the team were first Dr Sandra Burr, and later Dr Monica Carroll, each of whom brought their own expertise in poetry and cultural research to support the project.

We chose to focus on poetry because it is a mode of literary art that to a considerable extent stands outside the broad literary field. Other genres and modes of writing are, by and large, committed to communication, whether of ideas, story or information. Poetry, by contrast, deals with the ineffable, with that which resists or escapes codification; and hence it engages with sensory aspects and imagery rather than with narrative. It is also perhaps the least instrumental of all literary modes: it has a very minor presence in the curriculum, compared with, say, fiction; and there is neither a popular audience nor large-scale market-oriented production for contemporary English-language poetry. The several reports produced by cultural economist David Throsby bear this out, for Australian poets at least. His most recent reports, published in 2015, show that poetry has virtually no footprint in the larger publisher category, but relies on small and micro-publishers and therefore experiences a more limited distribution network than do children's books, literary and genre fiction, and creative nonfiction (Throsby, Zwar and Morgan 2018). Not surprisingly, therefore, poets receive the lowest income of all Australian writers, by a substantial margin: the average gross income from writing in the 2013/2014 financial year reached only $4,000 for poets, compared with $12,900 for all writers (Zwar, Throsby and Longden 2015).

Despite this apparent condition of deficit in the art form, there is a substantial population of poets across the world, possessed of substantial social, intellectual and cultural capital. On the whole, poets are highly educated, reflexive and engaged individuals whose poetry, prose, and knowledge-transfer practices add considerable value to their communities. And despite their comparative exclusion from the world of money and social recognition, they keep producing poetry, keep connecting with other poets, writers and scholars, and show considerable skill in innovation and in community building. What Pierre Bourdieu describes as poetry's 'emancipation ... from the rule of money and interest' (2010: 222) seems to have resulted in a very strong drive to create for its own sake, while other fields of creative endeavour, particularly business and science, are necessarily equally motivated by the need to generate a financial or knowledge return.

In the rest of this essay, drawing on several of our earlier publications and on some fresh analyses of the data, we set out the framework for the project, and then move to its key findings. First we discuss findings that illustrate the context for poetic 'excellence' – which, for the purposes of this project, we define as work that is both influential in the field, and widely recognised. We move on to explicate the formative moments, individuals and institutions that ensured the poets were 'switched on' to their art form; and finally we consider the role of collaboration, connection and community in the development of high-quality and sustained creative practice. These sections draw on conference presentations and publications produced by Carroll and Webb during the course of the project, and reviewed again before rehearsing the key issues in this volume.

The project: Understanding creative excellence: A case study in poetry

In 2013, the ARC provided funding for a project designed to investigate creativity by means of a case study of contemporary poets. Specifically, the project addressed not the poetry, but the poets themselves. Investigations were aimed at documenting elements of each poet's biography and practice including:

- where/how the poet grew up;
- biographical influences;
- connections to community;
- connections to the poetry sector;
- specific conditions of how poetic work is conceived and created; and
- poetic aims, hopes, and achievements.

In short, the project brief was to examine the poets' habitus in relation both to the sub-field of poetry, and the broader socio-economic field in which they dwell.

Over 2014–15, the research team recruited and then interviewed around 80 poets from nine different nations; each poet was identifiably in one of three key stages in their poetry career. The criteria in choosing respondents for interview were, simply:

(a) they write in English, so we could read their own words without translation; and

(b) they consider themselves, at some level, to be a poet.

The selection of respondents was not 'scientific', and this study therefore tells a great deal about those who participated, but cannot be directly translated into a statistical and fully representative account of the population of poets. However, it does provide good coverage of the field of Anglophone poets and this, enhanced by biographical and other study, gives us confidence that it paints a reasonable portrait of how children first become captivated by poetry, and then begin to craft a life in poetry.

We began by drawing on our collective expertise of the contemporary Anglophone community of poets to produce a list of preliminary potential respondents. We tested the list among ourselves and then with other experts in Australia and abroad. In the list we aimed to include poets practicing in a variety of key forms. This included poets working in one or more forms incorporating:

- the conventional form, the lyric;
- conceptual forms such as the l-a-n-g-u-a-g-e poets; and/or
- those committed to visual and material poetics in their work.

We aimed also to include, as far as possible, meaningful proportions of key demographics including gender, age and nationality. This resulted in a respondent cohort that included women and men, a range of ages, and a variety of national origins. We also chose, from within each nation, respondents in both urban and regional or rural locations. In a few cases, one or other of the interviewers had a prior professional or social acquaintance with the respondent, but for the most part we knew each other only through our publications.

After the first tranche of interviews, in year 2014, and under the direction of Michael Biggs, we followed a Delphi method of examining both the design of the project and the findings to date. Following the outcome of this examination, in 2015 we made a point of recruiting more early career and lesser-known poets, and expanded the schedule of questions slightly, but otherwise needed to make few changes to our process.

The methodology was based on a constructivist, interpretive approach to research. Of the four formal investigators, three are poets and three are also cultural theorists, so our research was both internal (poets talking to poets) and external (social researchers analysing the outcomes of poets talking to poets). What we hoped to find out was whether, based on qualitative data, there are any measurable differences between poets who are very successful and all the others. Are highly 'creative' people – creative in inverted commas, meaning those who are particularly effective at making and presenting their creative work – are they just born lucky? Do the contexts of their upbringing and education make a difference? Do they work harder and longer than everyone else? Have they hit on an approach to poetry that consistently delivers excellent results?

Our project enters the conversation at this gap, with our aim being to investigate poetry as a culture (or sub-field) with its own structures, processes, histories and modes of practice; and to investigate poets rather than either poems or their readers. We attempted to tease out, in research conversations, the selected poets' personal histories, the ways in which they identify their subject positions, their connections to the national and international community of poets, and their modes of operation. By the end of 2015 we had 75 useable transcripts of interviews (one interview was with two poets, so there are 76 individuals represented in the corpus – see **Table 1**). The interviews ranged from about 45 minutes to about two hours, and thus the transcripts totalled nearly a million words. To facilitate the interpretation of all this material, we decided to use NVivo, a software program designed to support the clustering and analysis of qualitative data.

We organised the cohort of poet-respondents according to three categories. The first, Group 1, comprises poets who are recognisable 'household names': those who have a very significant public profile, are cited widely both within and outside the community of poetry, have won internationally recognised honours, and hence have significant influence within the community of poetry. Group 2 comprises poets who have achieved national

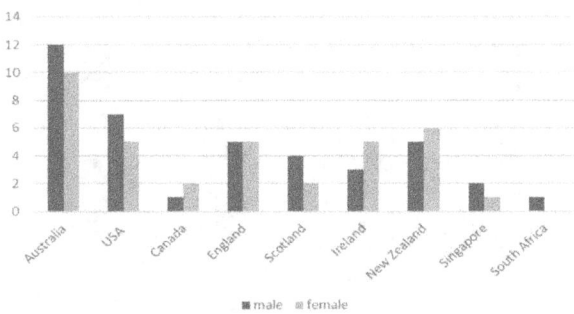

Table 1: *The poets in the project (n=76)*

recognition; and Group 3 includes both poets whose practice operates primarily at a local level, and those who are beginning to test out their creative identity. We should stress that the poets interviewed were allocated to groups not because their poetry was necessarily significantly 'better' or more 'creative' than the poets in the other two groups; rather, it was predicated on the visibility of each poet and their publications, and hence their level of influence over how poetry is understood within and beyond poetry circles.

The ARC project has been completed and the funding acquitted, and the investigators have published a number of articles on the findings. However, the work is not yet concluded: the data continues to demand our attention, and we therefore continue to analyse the transcripts and related information. This includes reviewing the established knowledge about the habitus of creative

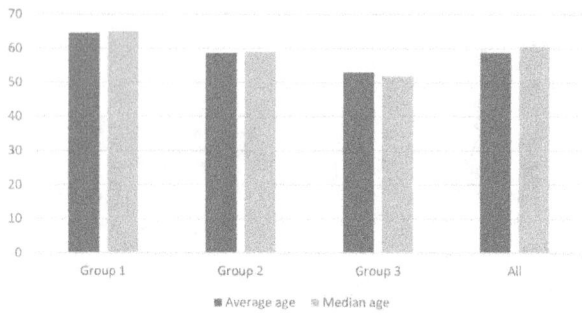

Table 2: *Age range for poets in the study (n=76)*

practitioners and the processes they deploy to compete for a position within the field, while hoping to illuminate the conditions and contexts associated with significant creative potential.

Characteristics of highly successful poets

Certainly we had expected to find some differences between Group 1 poets and the others, but we had no preconceptions about what those differences might be. After analysis of the data, it was clear that there are five key areas in which the Group 1 cohort really did show measurable differences from their colleagues in the other two groups. The first distinction is age (see **Table 2**): while the poets as a whole have an age range of 33 to 86 years, the highly successful poets are typically older (poetry is a slow game). Poets in this cohort span 43 to 82 years, with a median age of 65, while the median for the other two groups is 59 (Group 2) and 51 (Group 3).

The second distinction is that Group 1 poets are, almost universally, embedded in their community of practice (see **Table 3**, overleaf). Not all poets responded clearly to the questions here, but of the 66 who did make explicit comments, it is clear that they are distinguished by cohort. The connections of poets in Group 1 to other poets and to the poetry sector begins early in their careers, with active membership of writing groups, and then they remain part of that community throughout their careers. While a number of this group no longer participate in a writing group, all remain connected to the sector; and none identify themselves as solitary now or in the past. Many of them report attachments to a few writing friends, describing these relationships as both current and long-sustained friendships that, presumably, provide mutual support and galvanise each other's practice, in comments such as: 'those people are very important to my poetry practice', and 'We've worked together for 15 or 16 years now'.

The third key area addresses the level of education (see **Table 4**, overleaf). On the whole, all poets in the study are very well educated, with a remarkable 41 of the 76 individuals holding doctorates, and only three having completed their education at secondary school level. This is well aligned with the Australia Council for the Arts evidence that artists generally 'are among the most highly educated professionals in Australia' (2015: 16). But the poets of international renown, Group 1, are better educated than most: all

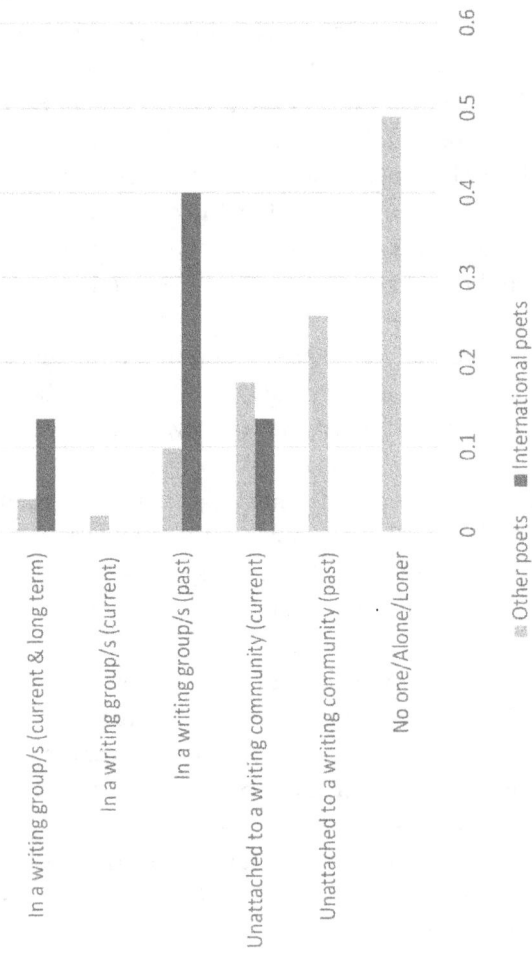

Table 3: *Attachments, by category of poet (n=66)*

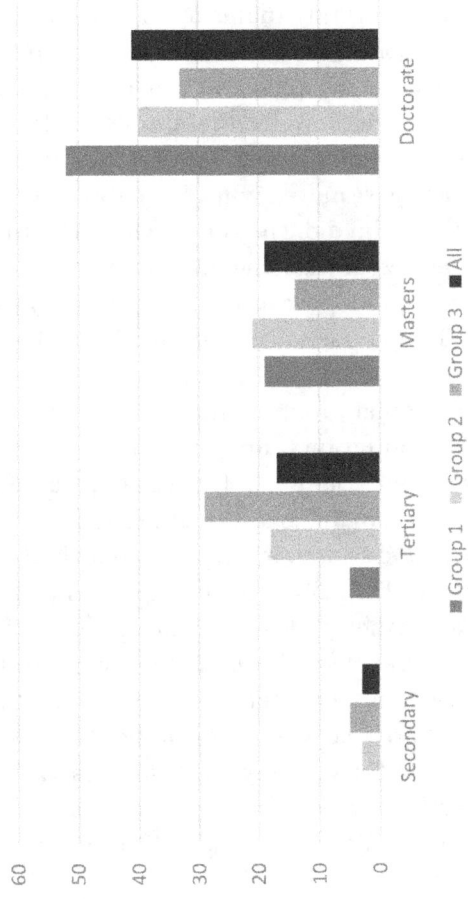

Table 4: *Education levels attained* (%)

have completed at least an undergraduate degree, and over 50% hold doctorates.

The fourth key area explores the relation of the poets and their practice to their geographical location. Interestingly, none of the poets seem particularly mobile; only 11 of the 76 are currently living in a nation or region that is not, or not near, their place of birth. However, the international poets are even less peripatetic than the group as a whole. Fewer of them have moved from their nation of birth; most of those who did, emigrated while they were still children; by contrast, the transnational poets in the other two groups are as likely to have migrated as adults. Group 1 poets also tend not to move house or home but have put down roots, compared with poets in the other groups, who are more likely to have been immigrants, and/or to move around within their own country. This does not mean that Group 1 poets remain doggedly close to home: they travel often, and widely, but typically only for brief trips – going on holidays, or travelling for workshops, festivals and other professional engagements. We have no data to explore why this is. However, we infer from observation, conversation and experience that their comparative geographic stability has allowed them to devote time, energy and resources to their poetic practice, rather than being distracted by the stress, expense, disconnection, and effort involved in relocation.

Finally, we come to the issue of gender (see **Table 5**). While close to fifty per cent of the poets

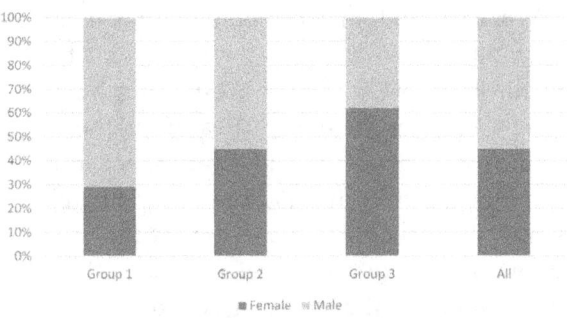

Table 5: *Status of poets by gender (%)*

interviewed are women, they make up only thirty per cent of Group 1, the internationally renowned poets category. The project team attempted to recruit in accordance with gender balance but, as the data shows, poetry is characterised by the same pattern of gendered access that is evident in other fields of endeavour. It is more difficult for women to attract the sort of attention and recognition that is available to men operating in the same field and at the same general level. While the creative sector has come a long way, in terms of gendered practice, so that some of the structural processes of exclusion highlighted in Linda Nochlin's seminal essay 'Why have there been no great women artists' (Nochlin 1988) no longer hold sway, there are still significant and systemic gendered differences in access to publishers, access to major publishers, access to prizes and honours, and access to reviews (see Weinberg & Kapelner 2018; Shamsie 2015).

What we find, in these data, is that there is a measurable difference between the Group 1 poets and those of national or local standing; and that perhaps the most significant feature is the extent to which, as individuals, they are embedded in the creative community. There are, however, a number of features that seem to be consistent with the poetic habitus, no matter the level of recognition they have attained. In the following sections we discuss findings across the whole corpus of interviews, considering three features: how poetry first captured the attention of those who were to become poets; the role of the education system in switching on the poetic habitus; and a more extensive discussion of the role of the community.

From child to poet: The role of memory

One of the questions each poet was asked was: 'when did you first encounter poetry?' We had included this in the schedule of questions first because of the very old, and commonly expressed, notion that poets are born with a penchant for poetry; and next, because of our researched-based intuition that those who go on to become established poets would have recognised poetry – or been recognised by it – at an early age. The aphorism applied here is expressed as *poeta nascitur, non fit*: the poet is born, not made.[1]

---

[1] The source of the aphorism is uncertain; it may have been first presented in Pseudo-Acro's commentary on Horace (c.200), but it is

Especially among those commentators who are themselves successful writers, this aphorism is accepted in a largely unexamined manner. Jack Kerouac, for instance, claimed that 'geniuses of the writing art ... are born', but everyone else is made (1995: 488), while Mary Oliver opens her *Poetry Handbook* with the assertion, 'Everyone knows that poets are born and not made in school' (1994: 1).

But being born with a penchant for something is not the end of the story. No writer emerges out of a blank space: everyone has to be introduced, somehow, to the possibility of writing, and has to come to see themselves as a member of the community of writers. The nineteenth-century medical specialist Robert Fletcher, in his article 'The Poet – is he born, not made?', draws on Philip Sidney's *Apologie for Poetry* when he agrees that poets must be born with the 'divine oestrum'; but continues:

> You cannot by any known process of training or teaching make a poet of a man without this birthright; but it is equally true that the higher the teaching bestowed upon him, the broader the field of operation opened to him, the greater becomes the poet in proportion; and not only that, but it may be asserted that without such training, be it greater or less, the divine gift mostly comes to nought. (1893: 118)

more likely to be the product of a seventh century compilation, and then rehearsed over the subsequent centuries until it became 'true', as aphorisms are true (Ringler 1941: 498).

We must have input from others, agrees author Wayne Macauley, who says he began writing 'under the influence of a teacher' who 'energised whatever was in my head' (in Wood 2016). Born, *and* made. Because after all, if there had been nothing in his character to begin with, nothing would have been energised.

Table 6 shows the responses by each group, and by the whole cohort, to the question of when they first came across poetry. Of the poets in the study, 67 provided a response, and they divide quite evenly across the three groups. In this table we present their responses by percentage; each set sums to more than 100% because most poets provide more than one account of their 'first encounter': when they first noticed that poetry was a particular use of language; when they were first captivated by poetry; and when they began to think of themselves as practitioners in the form.

Overall a majority of the poets remember first recognising poetry as a different mode of language use before they even reached school. This they attribute to living in a bookish household with parents or grandparents who were keen on poetry; and/or to having caregivers who read them nursery rhymes and similar rhythmic material; and/or to their experience of church – typically, a liturgical church – where the cadences and diction of sixteenth-century English began to inflect their sense of what language can do.

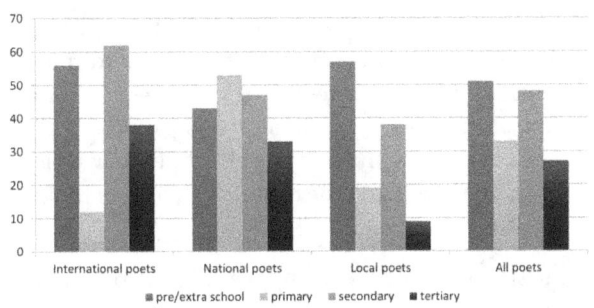

Table 6: *Stage of schooling where poetry was first encountered (%) (n=67)*

The next period of encounter is primary school, and some 32% of poets report being exposed to poetry at this stage. Notably, the internationally recognised poets offered very little comment on their primary school experience. Some said there was no poetry in their primary school experience; others said that while they did come across poetry there, it was 'in a minor way', and it was badly taught. We suspect, on the basis of their responses to other questions as well as this 'first encounter' question, that because so many of this group had encountered poetry early, the primary school curriculum and its teachers had little impact on them; that they found it neither fresh nor demanding. Most of them therefore had to wait for high school and, as the table shows, a majority of them identify secondary education as the point where they encountered poetry as more than a discrete language mode, but as a mode that deeply caught their attention. Poet B81, for example, recalls:

> at A level stage we had to study *The Wasteland* and I just remember finding it an extraordinarily exciting poem. I remember the teacher ... reading the poem as well, I remember being quite mesmerised by that very flat Eliot delivery which somehow added to the drama rather than took the drama away.

What the data seems to suggest is that pre-school and/or primary school encounters alerted the poets to this particular, even peculiar, use of language; and then high school is the point most of them remember as the key moment for their connection to poetry – for moving them from a mere meeting with the form to being switched on to it, or investing in it. Says Poet A19: 'I remember a particular English teacher slapping Prufrock down in front of us and not being able to make head or tail of this . . . but knowing there was something there that was incredibly interesting'. For Group 1 poets, and to a lesser extent Group 2 poets, tertiary education is the point they recall as their true entry to poetry: where they deeply connected with poetry and understood that they belonged to the form, or it to them.

Table 7 re-examines this data, incorporating both tertiary education and adult life experience of encountering poetry, and collapsing Groups 2 and 3 into a single category in order to examine the difference between poets who have attained an international reputation, and those who have not.

Clearly, Group 1 poets seem to have taken longer than the other poets to encounter poetry – or rather,

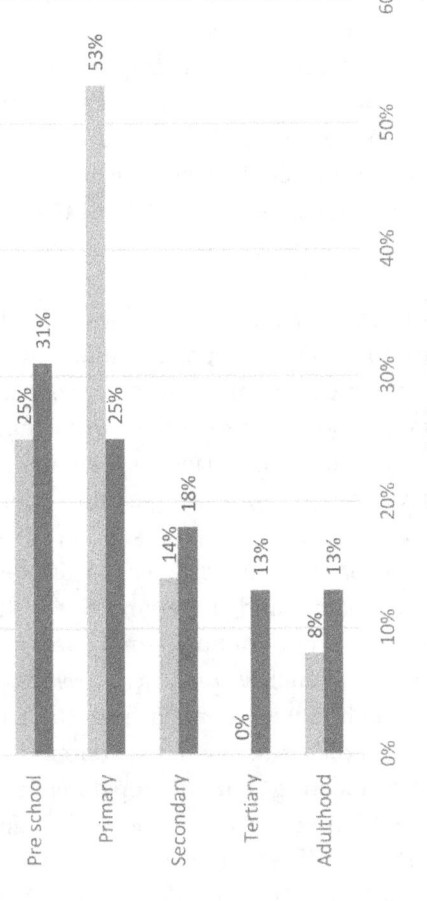

Table 7: *Reported age of first encounter.*
Comparing age at first encounter between categories of poet (%) (n=67)

they do not recollect poetry as being important until they were adolescents. While 78% of poets in Groups 2 and 3 remembered having encountered poetry by primary school, only 56% of Group 1 poets remember this experience. Even at the end of secondary school, Group 1 poets are lagging: only 74% of them report having encountered poetry by this stage, compared with 92% of the other poets. But, significantly, only Group 1 poets remember university as the point where they encountered poetry; and for post-secondary experience as a whole, 26% of Group 1 poets, and only 8% of the other poets, remember a connection.

This seems counter-intuitive, but we consider there is a reason for this self-reporting, and that the reason lies in the meaning of the word 'encounter'. Arguably, Group 1 poets simply did not pay much attention to their early experiences of listening to nursery rhymes and hymns, or reading poetry at primary and even secondary school. Their characterisation of these experiences is as mere 'meetings' with poetry; and the etymology of the word *encounter* does not connote simply 'meet'. It comes from the Old French *encontre*, a *confrontation*; and the Old French is itself derived from the Late Latin *incontra* – *in* plus *against*. An encounter, then, is not a neutral meeting, but a compelling, even adversarial event; and the Group 1 poets certainly did not report their 'first' or 'real' meeting with poetry as neutral. When they describe hearing poetry when they were small children, mentioning nursery rhymes, or the Anglican liturgy in church, these are mild engagements. By contrast, they describe their first genuine connection to poetry as a moment of being electrified by the form.

Poet A16, for instance, said that when he was at school, poetry 'meant absolutely nothing to me. It was taught very badly'; but that when he encountered it later, he was enthralled. The data needs to be read in this light: this is a poet who actually met poetry as a very young child but rejected it until after he had finished a BA in literature. His real point of entry was not the education system, but a friend who introduced him to the work of a particular poet. He continues:

> it was only much, much later on, when all this schooling was over – I hated my school days – before I actually began to realise there was something in poetry. I began by delving into Gerard Manley Hopkins … My friend just gave me the Penguin anthology and said, 'You should read that.' I remember reading the most difficult poem he'd written, 'The Wreck of The Deutschland', and feeling completely and utterly at sea but knowing that there was a music there that I needed to touch.

It was in meeting Hopkins through the agency of a friend, and being excited by the form and the music, that poetry came alive to him, and he fell in love with it.

As **Table 8** shows (overleaf), Group 3 poets, those who are just starting out or have a local profile, have

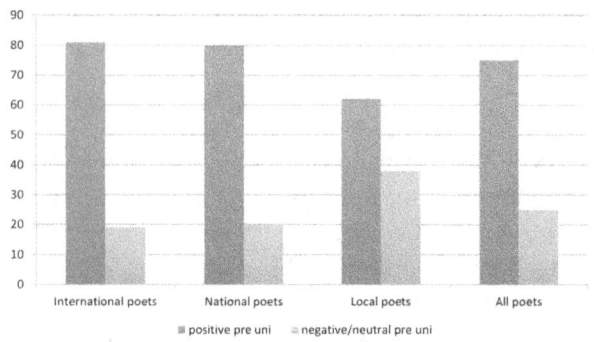

Table 8: *Reported experience of first encounter prior to tertiary education (%) (n=67)*

less happy memories than do poets in either Group 1 or Group 2, which suggests that the education system has the capacity to depress as well as enthuse proto-poets. However, the poets as a whole do remember their school experience as being generally positive.

As noted above, we had intuited that the education system would have been important in 'switching on' children to poetry, but the majority of the poets report that they first came across poetry at home, albeit only as a 'meeting', and not an encounter. Table 9 shows that family members are the second highest category of 'matchmakers' for poetry, and while various family members were mentioned, mostly grandparents and mothers took on the role of introducing their children to the form (this is not surprising, given that mothers and grandparents are more likely to have primary care of pre-schoolers). After family come teachers, and

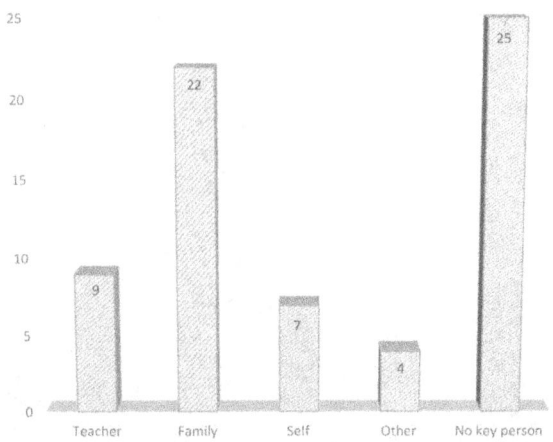

Table 9: *The matchmaker*
Significant person mentioned as part of first encounter (n=67)

then 'Self' – referencing the poets whose memory of first meeting is when they read a poem and were captivated by it – and then 'Other' – those poets who report bumping into poetry through the media or in some other guise.

Where **Table 9** becomes confusing, or at least offers unexpected findings, is the surprisingly high number of respondents who claimed that there was no specific point of reference, no person or institution who introduced them to poetry. This seems at odds with what we had noted in the previous tables. But **Table 10** (overleaf) illuminates the issue: all poets in Group 1 can remember the moment they first encountered poetry, and with whom. What this suggests is that almost half of the poets in the other

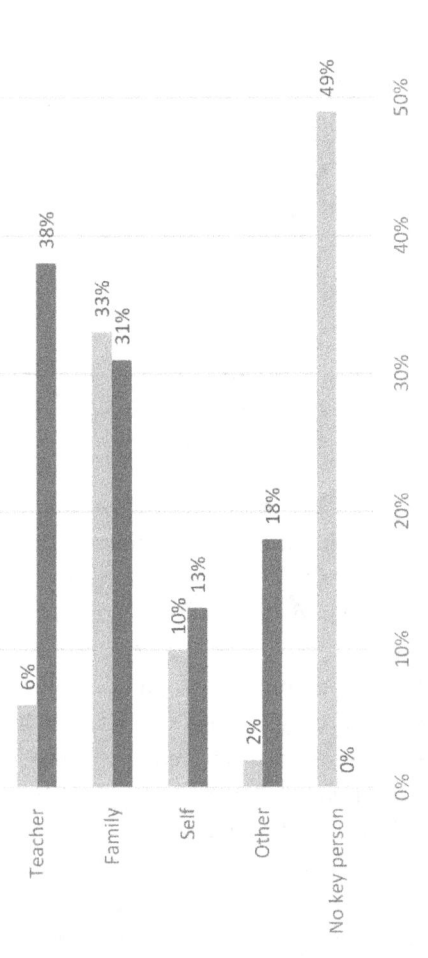

Table 10: *The role of the matchmaker, by group of poets*
Comparing key person at first encounter between categories of poets (n=67)

two groups remember coming across poetry, but the detail of those meetings did not sear itself on their memory.

A second point that emerges from **Table 10** is that though the Group 1 poets remember the school environment as being comparatively irrelevant, their school teachers were influential: for 38% of them, it was a teacher who effected their introduction, compared with only 6% of the other poets. We wondered, here: did the proto Group 1 poets pay more attention in school? Probably not, given their dismissive comments on the introduction of poetry in class. What is more likely is that certain teachers recognised their potential, and paid more attention to those pupils. Poet A11 recalls: 'in the lower stages of secondary school we had an English teacher who was very interested in poetry'. This teacher introduced her to the work of Adrian Mitchell which, she says, 'would have been very modern in those days'. This was not her first introduction; she reported reading a range of other poems and poets at home and at primary school, including John Heath-Stubbs, Walter de la Mare, John Keats et al., but it was her secondary school teacher who facilitated her encounter with poetry, and at it was at this point that the rhythm and colour in poetry began to make real sense to her.

An introduction, as noted above, does not necessarily equal an encounter; and what **Table 11** (overleaf) shows is that nearly all the introductions were simply that: moments when the young proto-

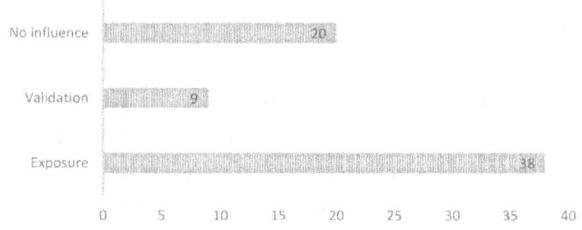

Table 11: *Type of influence of significant person (n=67)*

poets were exposed to poetry – possibly a formative point in the development of their poetic habitus, but with little actual influence on how they engaged with the form. For well over half, it was simply exposure to the form; for almost a third, the blunt response was that such exposure had no influence on their later fascination with poetry. Where it becomes interesting is the small proportion of the poets – only 9 of the 67, or 13% – who remember their matchmaker having validated their interest in poetry.

Again, this differs between groups (see **Table 12**). For Group 1 poets, their exposure to and validation by their matchmaker is more significant than it is for all the others, who simply remember that there was a someone somewhere who opened a door: 35% of them report that their key person had no influence on their entry into poetry. Group 1 poets, though, are more likely to remember the encounter moment quite vividly; and only a very small proportion of them say that this moment had no influence on them.

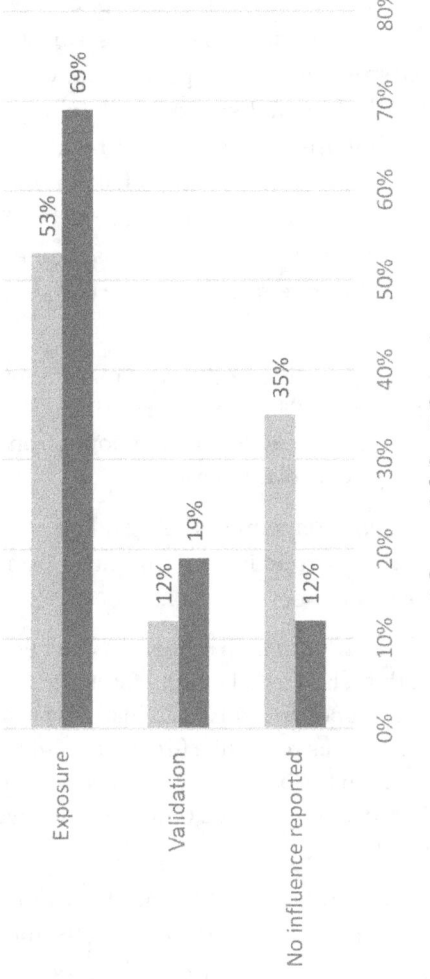

Table 12: *Type of influence of significant person, by category*
Comparing role of key person between categories of poets (%) (n=67)

Personal validation pays an important role. Group 1 poets by a significant margin – 20%, compared with only 12% of the other poets – vividly remember their 'matchmaker' taking seriously their own early attempts at writing poems. Not only were they validated to a higher extent than were the other poets, but the exposure they recall is both more positive and more impactful. Poet A14, for example, gives quite an extended narrative of how she was introduced to poetry by a teacher, ending up by reciting the poem that was part of that first encounter:

> 'You've hurt your finger? Puir wee man! Your pinkie? Deary me!' I remember reciting it and that somehow, I can't quite remember how, I won a tin of Cadbury's chocolates for it.

Poet B80 similarly remembers being taken seriously by a teacher, and that it was this attention that switched her on to poetry:

> it wasn't really until high school ... a teacher spotted that I had a real affinity for it and gave me an extra book to read ... and instantly I was like boom. It was really like fireworks going off somewhere in the back of my brain because I'd never heard language used that way and it was a real instant kind of ignition.

Memory is a central element in the stories many of the poets tell, but for the emerging poets, the memory is often vague, or is not particularly personalised. Take poet C12, for example:

> I remember how emotional people were when they were reciting poetry. Now a lot of the poetry of my childhood would have been political poetry, typical kind of Irish nationalist political poetry: ballads of Feinians and ballads of heroes, of dead heroes. So I think it was the emotion I could perceive in my elders as they recited. Obviously reciting this stuff meant something to them. That I remember most. And also I remember the love people had of rhyming, you know? When the clack, the cluck of the rhyme came through, people loved remembering the rhymed word.

This is beautifully recalled, but is very general in terms of the narrative. By contrast, poet A18 remembers that, discounting his hearing of Mother Goose and similar rhymes:

> the first poems I consciously remember are 'Crossing the Line', *Archy and Mehitabel*, and the great rhythmic poems, like 'How they brought the good news from Ghent to Aix', 'The Highwayman'. Things like that stick in your head. But the first time I really got interested was my last year of high school, and we had a teacher over those last two years of high school, and it started with Keats, really, and the Romantics; and then in Year 12 the teacher [introduced me to] Yeats. It was the first time I'd heard Yeats, and that was like a bell tolling in my head ... it astonished me – how did he do that? And Eliot, I still remember – what aroused me then was utter puzzlement: I still remember 'Let us go then you and I, when the evening is spread out against the sky like a

patient etherized upon a table'. I still remember thinking 'Like what?' But you never get those lines out of your head.

This poet exemplifies what turns up again and again in the transcripts: many of the poets, and almost without exception all the Group 1 poets, date their exposure, their first encounter, from a particular moment of grace, a moment of recognition, where suddenly poetry came alive to them. They vividly recall that moment, often naming the poem itself and very often going on to recite bits of it. It is an *a-ha* moment, a moment of falling absolutely in love with the form. And, for them, it is an enduring and intense memory.

We cannot evaluate the accuracy of those memories, or to what extent they have been shaped and coloured by the lives they have lived after that seminal moment. But for the poets describing their entry to the field, it is something they hold close: both the remembering of that moment and the poems associated with it, and the recognition they believe they had for poetry at that moment, and it had for them.

Teachers of influence: Switching on the poet

School may not matter, in the making of a poet who starts early and builds a sustained career; but teachers matter. Moving through the chronology of creativity within each biography traced in this

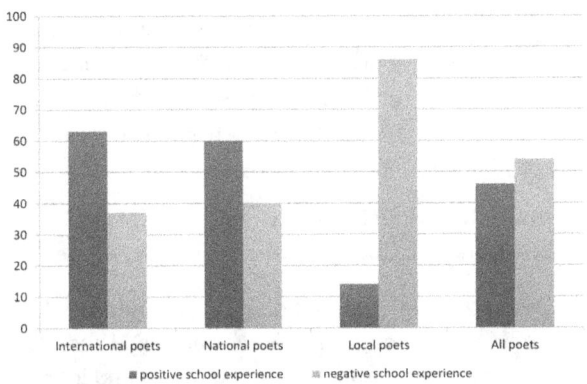

Table 13: *What happened in the classroom? Reported quality of first encounter at school (%) (n=67)*

project, we find that there is something going on in the realm of formal education that involves teachers and the school curriculum at primary and secondary levels, and across all nine nations in which we recruited participants.

What is startling in the data is that the poets who have not, or not yet, blossomed into their poetry careers (Group 3) remember school as an inhibiting space, while the other two groups overall have a far more positive memory of its affordances. But while the international and national poets are almost identical in their reporting of whether school was positive or negative, there is a difference in the language they use to describe it and hence to code their own sense of their life and its trajectories. Nearly 20% of the international poets use the word 'luck' or 'lucky' to describe what school gave them, for their poetry careers; only 10% of the national poets use that word, and only 5% of the local poets. They tend, too, to describe those important teachers in highly positive terms; for example:

> Poet A20: 'when I was in Grade 10, I was just really lucky to have a brilliant English teacher.'

> Poet A22: 'Mrs Ledley, P6: she was fabulous. Mrs Ledley first brought in poems and read them out to the class and then told us to go and learn them and say them, and that was an electrifying experience for me.'

> Poet B47: 'I don't remember studying poetry until high school. Then I just lucked out and had a fantastic teacher who turned me on to Wallace Stevens.'

> Poet B65: 'I was very lucky, I had a very good English teacher who had a big effect. You know, there was always that kind of figure. There was an English teacher who, I think, recognised I had some talent, who was the one who, in many ways, transformed my life.'

> Poet A11: 'I was very lucky because in the lower stages of secondary school we had an English teacher who was very interested in poetry'

> Poet A17: 'I had one English teacher when I was at high school who was really interested in poetry and who read stuff that I was writing when I was just starting and he was pretty encouraging.'

The poets in Group 3 do not remember this sort of relationship with teachers, and nor do they report the 'luck' that is appreciated by their colleagues in Groups 1 and 2. What is fascinating here is that the 'successful' poets seem to attribute that success to something outside their own efforts: not the sort of logic associated with classic capitalist self-construction, but rather a sense of grace received.

One of the arguments mounted in the extant literature for how individuals achieve their aptitude is the 'born not made' logic we discuss above; this relies on the notion that personality and, by extent, habitus, is coded by an individual's genetic makeup, and therefore more important that are the other factors that have been identified as part of sociopolitical or cultural participation. Poet and political scientist Jeffrey Mondak writes:

> Although there may not be a genetic marker for participation . . . it may be that genes directly influence extraversion, conscientiousness, and agreeableness, along with corresponding connections between these traits and the individual's likelihood of becoming an active participant in local politics. (2010: 46)

Key factors, he writes, are time, money and other resources; intrinsic interest; or being mobilised by someone else (2010: 151).

A second line of thought comes from avant-garde logic, and is associated with a series of experiments that draw analogies between genetic coding and art (Sommerer & Mignonneau 2015; Müller-Funk

2012). Christa Sommerer and Laurent Mignonneau identify text as a 'genetic code' for artificial creatures (2015: 315) and extrapolate from that what they call 'living poetry': artwork which, designed through the combination of 'genetic programming techniques, interactivity, and experimental literature', produces a new form of poetry (2015: 318). Writers who share this perspective are very likely to reference the Austrian avant-garde artist HC Artmann, and his EightPoint Proclamation of the Poetical Act, the first of which reads: 'There is one statement which is irrefutable, namely that one can be a poet without having so much as written or spoken a single word' (in Müller-Funk 2012: 211).[2]

While the first perspective focuses on internal and external forces in the history of the production of an artist, the second focuses on the production of the artist through practices of art. We accept both these views, but argue that while one's genetic coding provides a predisposition, it needs to be switched on, and nourished, so that it will become part of the habitus of the individual. What switches us on as children is, generally, either/both the family environment and the school environment; and as both Table 3 and Australia Council reports show, poets are generally possessed of the sort of habitus that generates in them dispositions to seek and attain education. The poets who participated in this

---

[2] We cannot access the original German for Artmann's proclamation, so have to rely on this secondary reference.

project, and especially the 67 who provide expansive and explicit discussions about how they came into poetry, make it clear that poets are 'born', but they are also 'made': their predisposition needs to become part of the structuring structures of the habitus, and family and home life are both very important in providing a positive introduction to the world of poetry. School then begins the process of separation between those who will flourish, and those who will edge toward or around the edges of the sub-field of poetry. This suggests first that personality – the poet's own genetic coding – is vital in setting the stage for the initial recognition of/by poetry, and for the way they respond to teacher engagement; and next, that curriculum content, and teacher engagement, are vital in firing up the poet or in depressing their experience of the form. What we consider now is what matters – what has effect – once poets are past the immediate influence of family and education.

Myth of the lone poet[3]

The philosopher PZ Brand (2015) raises an important problem for studies of creativity, one that has particular resonance for poets. This is the depiction of the creative identity as both rare and highly individual. We see this in the many popular portrayals of the brilliant scientist/writer/artist

---

[3] This section draws on our previous publication, J Webb and M Carroll (2017) 'A seethe of poets: Creativity and community', *TEXT Special Issue 40* (April).

who is always on the edge of the group: who works alone and makes contributions well above the capacity of ordinary people; and who pays for this excellence with poor social skills and limited human contact. Brand argues against this view of creative excellence, writing that the idea that creativity is tied to notions of originality, or creation based on individual mental processes, simply replicates the cultural bias towards the individual artist/genius.

We might suggest it is more than a cultural bias: that it is a trope with a very long history. This trope begins with Plato, who urged for solitude, and he was followed by centuries of philosophers and poets who equally insisted on this as a vital ingredient for high level thought and creativity. Psychologist Anthony Storr effectively flies a flag for this position in the title of his *Solitude: a return to the self*, in which he analyses biographical details of various creative individuals and finds that 'imaginative capacity tends to become highly developed in gifted individuals who, for one reason or another, have passed rather solitary childhoods' (1989: 106). He goes on to make the rather startling claim that 'the gifts which enable a person to become a writer can be set in motion by loss and isolation' (1989: 120); and that in any event 'creative people are used to solitude' (1989: 129). We see the same process of valuing isolation for its contribution to creativity in the writing of the Romantics (Wordsworth wandering lonely as a cloud), the Transcendentalists (Thoreau's silken web of solitude), and the Modernists (Hardy's 'madding crowd'). In the mid-twentieth century this view is still evident in the expressions of poets: just two examples are William Carlos Williams, who rejoices in being 'lonely, lonely' (1966: 3); and Adrienne Rich, who describes loneliness with a contained pleasure: as 'a plane rides lonely and level / on its radio beam, aiming / across the Rockies'; like 'the rowboat ice-fast on the shore / ... / that knows what it is' (1973: 20). As scientist and sci fi writer Isaac Asimov insists, 'The presence of others can only inhibit' creative work (2014). However, if we consider the material conditions of the lives of very 'creative' people, typically they have deep and rich relationships: think of Wordsworth, whose family home contained not only himself but his sister Dorothy, his wife Mary, and their six children; or Thoreau, whose friends the Emersons not only provided him with a cottage on Walden Pond, but subsequently gave him a home in their house. Martha Nussbaum points out that being 'fully social' is a significant contributor to being 'more fully capable of being alone – therefore of the exhilaration of solitary contemplation' (2001: 149). Which points us to the 'wisdom' of poets: consider William Cowper, who anticipated Nussbaum in his poem 'Retirement', a sequence of reflections on what matters, for a good life, and what poetry can afford:

> I praise the Frenchman, his remark was shrewd—
> How sweet, how passing sweet, is solitude!
> But grant me still a friend in my retreat,
> Whom I may whisper – solitude is sweet.
>   (1835: 163)

Periods of solitude are sweet, and enable rich creative work to be accomplished; but being invested in intimate and meaningful relationships is equally sweet, and perhaps equally necessary, for the individual who wants a productive creative life.

A second issue that emerges from both the practitioner and the research literature on creativity is the notion that it is necessarily and intimately tied to the imagination, and hence to individual genius. Elizabeth Cobb's early (1959) and influential study of the need for children to have periods of solitude in order to develop imagination and creative capacity is an important example of this view (Cobb 1977: 94), and Berys Gaut's survey of the philosophy of creativity demonstrates the extent to which it focuses on the psychological connections between creativity and imagination (Gaut 2010). The problem with this is that it relies on the argument that creativity is based in individual mental processes, rather than in material encounters and actions or engagement with practice. It returns to the notion that creative genius is innate; and found in individuals who are separated in various ways from the rest of society; and who are therefore both uncontaminated by everyday thought, and capable of genuine novelty.

This, the 'romantic' view of creativity (Sefton-Green 2000), is not supported by more contemporary research, or by an examination of practice. Those individuals we identify as the giants on whose shoulders we stand are, on close examination, simply individuals who are typically engaged in, and rely upon, collaborations with others. In some cases those collaborations are material and consensual, as when two or more people work together on a project, co-author works they publish under both names. In other cases it is what we might characterise as an imagined collaboration: where an individual engages closely with the work of someone they have never met – a relationship afforded only through access to their works. In either case, they are relationships that energises practice, and that weave the individual practitioners into a social and discursive network.

Vlad Glaveanu's publications incline to the truism, thoroughly canvassed in the literature, that creativity must be expressed before it can be said to exist in fact, and as such survives not in the original creator but in the community that acknowledged it (see Fischer, Giaccardi et al. 2005). Glaveanu's study, 'Creativity as Cultural Participation', makes the case for creativity as 'both individual and socio-cultural mainly because individuals themselves are socio-cultural beings' (Glaveanu 2011: 48). It is necessarily individual, because it is put into practice by individuals who themselves possess both the skills and the disposition to make creative contributions. But those individuals learn their skills through their context – no one is born able to write a poem – and their works will be evaluated and accepted (or not) as creative outputs by other people or institutions. Consequently, he concludes, 'Creativity is never a solitary affair' (2011: 61).

This directs us to the question of whether there can be said to be a community of poets. In the absence of a professional status of 'poet', or formally instituted schools of poetry, how such a group might be identified is unclear. Nor, as noted above, do poets have much of a public profile in the broader community. Because of this, and because of the 'romantic' notion of creativity that so permeates contemporary culture, we had assumed that poets would tend to be solitary, or have only attenuated relationships with other poets. We wondered, if there were such a thing as 'the community of poets', whether it might not be of the sort described by Alphonso Lingis: 'the community of those who have nothing in common' (1994: 10).

For Lingis, this is the disturbingly 'other' community that emerges when one probes below the 'common discourse of which each lucid mind is but the representative': the other community that is made up of those excluded from the mainstream. Poets are, of course, not 'other' as Lingis describes that category. They are well educated and, apparently, socially integrated. However, in their identity as poets they are in many ways excluded; or feel as though they are. This was indicated by their responses to one of the questions we asked participants of the study: whether they would be likely to name themselves as poets when asked 'what do you do?' in a social encounter. Most said they would be unlikely to do so, because when in the past they have named themselves as poets, the social situation becomes 'awkward'. That, of course, is a problem only when speaking to 'outsiders', those who do not inhabit the creative field; and the fact that they do distinguish between 'other poets' and 'everyone else' hints at the presence of at least an imagined community.

We pursued the idea of a community of poets, taking as a starting point for our framing of the issue Randall Collins' major sociological study of the community of philosophers. His study is far more expansive than ours, since it covers many hundreds of philosophers across several millennia and in a broad range of cultures (Collins 1987: 47). Nonetheless, we found a number of homologies between the two studies. An important homology is that, for both poets and philosophers, there is what we might call a story of origin: how they entered the field, and under whose guidance and authority. Collins describes this process of entering as the effect of 'master-pupil chains' (1989: 108) – relationships that initiate new members and, at times, new schools; and that ensure continuity of philosophy as a discipline, and of particular schools, across generations (1989: 110). He found that the most eminent philosophers also have the most relationships across two axes. With respect to the vertical axis, they link backward in time to their predecessors – their own 'masters' and who came before them; and link forward in time to their own pupils and to those yet to come, but who will read them, and cite them, and keep their work alive.

Poets in our study often acknowledge or gesture toward a similar sort of relationship – they are clearly influenced by their predecessors, and in many cases by contemporary but more experienced poets who take them under their wing. They tend not to characterise these as 'master-pupil' relationships, but to speak of apprenticeships, or mentorship: as with Poet A24: 'I'm a great believer in a kind of apprenticeship ... If that's properly done, I've seen people really flourish'; or Poet C27 'I think we do learn in an apprentice system, really'. The relationships between elder and initiate may be actual ones, in that a poet is in fact taught by a living poet or mentored by a poetry editor. They are often, though, imagined elder-initiate or master-pupil relationships, where a poet connected with the 'ancestors' in poetry rather than the 'elders'. WH Auden encourages this latter approach for emerging poets. Once they have passed the 'beginning' stage, he writes:

> The next stage for the young poet is to get a transference upon some particular poet, with whom he feels an affinity ... In imitating his Master, the young poet learns that, no matter how he finds it, there is only one word or rhythm or form that is the right one. (1995: 191)

The relationship that draws, or mentors, a person into poetry is an important one. Virtually all the poets we interviewed had an 'origin' story, where they recounted a moment where the door of the poetry world opened to them. In some cases this was a version of Auden's 'imagined' relationship when they read a particular poem or series of poems and found themselves captured by the other. For others it was a more organic relationship – from such examples as a school teacher who initiated them into the delights of poetry and has remained part of their circle only in memory, through to instances where an early relationship has extended through much of their lives. Unlike Collins' study, where 'dominance' is a significant feature of such relationships, among poets these relationships are characterised by philanthropy and generosity: their origin stories are often followed by expressions of deep affection for 'first loves', and a sense of being a 'keeper of the flame'. Entry into, and a position within the domain of poetry is therefore perceived less as a prize to be won through struggle, and more as an inheritance.

While there is a degree of community within the population of poets, there are also deep and profound differences between schools of poetry: between lyric and language poets, for example, or bush poets and experimental poets. Overall, however – and perhaps because the community of poets receives very little public attention – public imbroglios are rare; and generally speaking poets, like cats, either get on well, or avoid each other. But they are not the solitary genius of the romantic tradition. In the interviews we conducted for this research, we asked about their relationship to the field, and/or the community, of poetry. An analysis of the answers shows that the depth of attachment or involvement, and the duration of attachment and involvement, varies quite considerably, but in virtually every case at least some relationship to other poets, and to the field itself, was described.

One of the questions we put to the poets in our study was about their own chains of connection, and the answers fell on a spectrum from those who claim absolutely no relationship with other poets, to those who are deeply involved in a sustained way with the community of poets. The data the resulted from this question is instructive as to how the community of poets is organised: which is remarkably similar to that of the community of philosophers as mapped by Randall Collins (1989: 120). If we take the vertical axis, the Group 1 poets – individuals of renown – are demonstrably linked both forward and backward in time to a greater extent than are the other poets; they are more likely to be mentioned by their contemporaries, which suggests a capacity to influence or support younger poets. This interrogates the notion that there are high levels of isolation expressed by poets. In fact, there are structural differences in how isolation or connection are experienced and expressed, and particularly in regard to gender differences. **Table 14** reworks the data in **Table 3** by focusing on gender and attachments:

These data show that women have more, and more sustained, relationships than do men; they are less likely to be attached to a single writing companion, or to have a spouse who acts as their writing companion, than are men; and are more

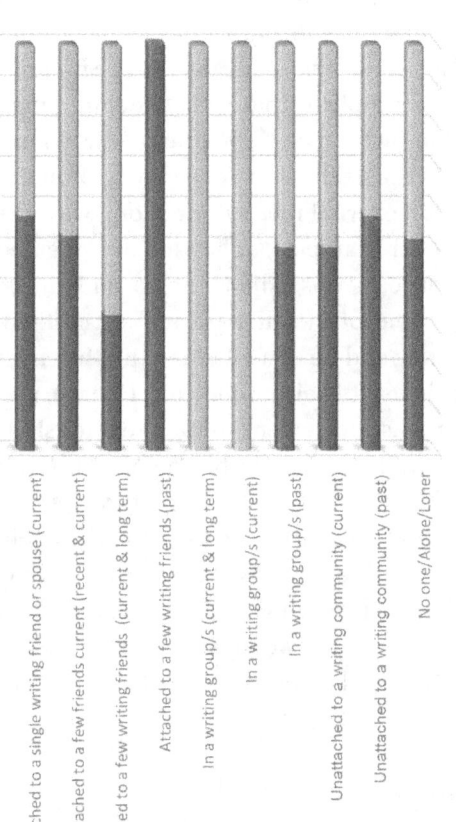

Table 14: *Gender and community attachments*
% *of gender answers, by categories of community attachment (100% stacked)*

likely to have longterm writing friends, and sustained involvement in writing groups. Finally, they are slightly less likely than are men to report isolation within the writing community.

But, on the whole, this study follows the findings of Collins' study to indicate that a creative community has connections in both past and present directions. For 'success' in the field – if by success we count the achievement of external recognition along with the affirmation of, for example, publication by esteemed publishing houses – it is important not only to be connected with a lot of other people in the field, but also to know and be connected with other high profile individuals. It is also important to have, and be able to demonstrate, elder / initiate relationships running in both directions; into the past, and into the future. This sort of social and cultural capital is inherited as much as it is earned: 'It is the chain itself, and the social conditions that make it possible, that elevates particular individuals into the status of the creative geniuses that we separate out for special treatment in our intellectual histories' (Collins 1989: 120).

The state of poetry

Although poetry is a very ancient art form, and one that receives formal recognition (insofar as it is often used to mark key moments in an individual's or a nation's life), and although it has practitioners and readers across the world, it produces what can only be described as a minor literature. Few of the people who write poetry achieve professional publication of their work, or maintain their writing practice across decades, and poetry has a miniscule economic footprint. It therefore achieves very little public coverage, has minimal impact on social, cultural and political events and, with respect to the cultural studies discipline, attracts little scholarly attention.

Poet and cultural theorist Rachel Blau DuPlessis suggests this latter issue is the result of 'the universalizing, taming, humanizing claims of poetry and the silvery aura around the word "poetic"', which represents poetry as both 'segregated ... from the social' (DuPlessis 2012: 53, 60), and apolitical. Maria Damon and Ira Livingston, similarly, posit that poetry has not been a good fit with cultural studies because it is embedded in the aesthetic, while the work of cultural studies is to 'politicize the aesthetic' (2009: 2, 6). While they encourage cultural studies scholars to take on questions of why particular people are moved or excited by an aesthetic object, this is not an approach that addresses questions of field. It positions poetry as of value for research, only insofar as it can be put to the work of understanding consumer engagement. Other contributors to Damon and Livingston's volume frame poetry as a space in which to examine the politics of gender, race and class, or in which social or political identities can be analysed. So in this, as in other cultural studies publications, poetry enters the conversation only when poems are framed as social, cultural or political artefacts, while the position of poets as social subjects, or of poetry as a socio-cultural practice, remains largely unaddressed.

The transcripts of our interviews produce a picture of a creative community we can think of as a 'culture', extrapolating from Deleuze and Guattari's designation of minor literature (1986: 16–17). The three criteria they identify for a minor literature are, first, that a minor literature is not the product of a minor language, but the product of a minority group operating within a major (dominant) culture; next, that minor literature is always political; and third, that the product of a minor culture is a collective one: 'there are no possibilities for an individuated enunciation that would belong to this or that "master" and that could be separated from a collective enunciation'. Clearly contemporary poetry does not precisely meet these criteria. English language poets in the early twenty-first century tend not to be members of an oppressed minority, but are well educated, often employed in a professional capacity, and typically well positioned to navigate the broader social field. Nor are they typically focused on a political enunciation: though, viewed from one perspective, everything done by a social subject is necessarily political, the data we have gathered point to poets whose primary concern is with the pulse of poetry, rather than with effecting political change. Perhaps most critically, these poets for the most part claim an 'individuated enunciation', rather than a collective one, and strongly assert ownership of their own utterances.

Nonetheless, there are features of Deleuze and Guattari's designation of minor culture that usefully delineate the space of contemporary poetry. First, because the poets use the major language to produce their minor literature, their poems present images and accounts of the world that are only loosely connected to mainstream images and accounts: they overlay the already-known, transport it elsewhere, and thus perform acts of deterrorialisation (Deleuze and Guattari 1987: 11). Further, as agents who simultaneously operate in the mainstream and reject the dominant logic of their day, they are outside mainstream culture. This is evident in the fact that many of them acknowledged that they would be unlikely to describe themselves as poets in the course of an ordinary social encounter, but instead identify as teacher, writer, editor. In some cases, they say, this is because they have found if they do declare themselves as poets, the social situation becomes 'awkward'; in other cases they say they would not name themselves 'poet' because it is more appropriate to say that they 'write poetry'. Generally, their descriptions of their experiences and understandings of the social framework is that they are indeed part of a minor culture and, though they have strong roots into the mainstream and move easily between the two, their 'belonging' is in poetry. The second criterion of a minor culture is that 'everything is political'. Though poets typically do not do double service as political activists, they are indeed political: first because their concerns are outward-facing, directed toward wider social issues than the purely personal; and next because they have chosen to operate in a field that offers little or no reward, and thus have refused the hegemony of neoliberal discourse. For Simon O'Sullivan (2005), this is characteristic of a minor practice: it instantiates a mode of resistance, whether expressed in active forms, or simply as a negation of the norm. This is evident, for O'Sullivan, in what they produce – which are objects that 'are not made for an already existing audience … They do not offer "more of the same". They do not necessarily produce "knowledge". They do not offer a reassuring mirror reflection of a subjectivity already in place' (O'Sullivan 2012: 4). Poetry fits this category because very little is written for a commercial audience: many of the poets we interviewed name themselves as their own first reader, their privileged audience. Nor are they are interested in reproducing earlier work: they aim to develop and expand, they strain to reach the ineffable, and to grasp the unthought, the unsaid. Perhaps because they are making a virtue of necessity, they are not concerned with material outcomes from their work, whether this takes the form of knowledge or of trade; and they aim to interrogate and transform subjectivity, rather than rehearse it.

Deleuze and Guattari's third criterion, the production of a collective rather than individual enunciation, seems at first blush to be entirely incommensurate with the 'minor culture' of poetry. However, a collective logic, and shared values and practices, are evident across the group, which points to the presence of a community whose overarching enunciation – of who they are, of what poetry can afford – is indeed a collective one. O'Sullivan (2005) suggests that this sort of creative community has a utopian function, being the 'precursor of a community (and often a nation) still in formation'. This does not align well with the concerns and determinations of the poets we interviewed, or with Foucault's description of utopia as 'society itself in a perfected form, or else society turned upside down' and 'a placeless place' (Foucault 1986: 23). Poetry might be better described as an atopia in the sense used by Foucault, since it is indeed 'the non-place of language' (Foucault 1973: xvi, xix). Poetry-as-atopia also fits Derrida's depiction: the 'between-space', the generative place where opposites are opposed (Derrida 1987: 9); or that of Barthes, for whom it is the refuge, the unclassifiable space where it is possible to be other (Barthes 1979: 12). However, this is not a sufficient description of poetry, because though the poets may be citizens of a minor culture, for the most part they assert a deeply felt connection to their geographic or national topos, and describe themselves as phenomenologically connected to the world, and to their societies. They may visit the between-space, and operate professionally in the non-place, but they don't live there.

Perhaps, therefore, a better way to conceive of their social situation is heterotopia, in the way Foucault uses that term, because these poets simultaneously belong to their local communities and stand outside them. The space they occupy is 'other' to the norm; it is a counter-site that operates within but alongside the dominant forms; and it is a (potentially) disruptive operation because unlike other minor cultures – jazz music, for instance, which in Australia enjoys publicly funded radio channels – poetry has no formal place. Consequently, it tends to operate as a pop-up, disrupting the space of café or bookshop or bar, and then disappearing back into its no-place. When it does claim a physical space, like any heterotopia its 'system of opening and closing' may be penetrable, but the conditions for doing so are both stringent and arcane: as is the experience of many a surprised diner who finds themselves the unwitting audience of a poetry reading, or the browser who blunders into a book launch (Foucault 1986: 26). Poets report the lack of material presence, the lack of social recognition, and the general social awkwardness that comes with membership of a dispersed minor culture. Yet they remain deeply invested in this minor literature, and conscious of the scope and scale of the community of which they are part – a community that extends back to Sappho and the Psalmists, and looks forward to poetic practices not yet imagined.

Conclusion

Where this project leaves us is with some clarity about the state of poetry in the contemporary Anglophone world, and a great deal of curiosity about new directions in which the findings are pointing. This is particularly with respect, first, to patterns and practices of exposure and education, and next to the possibility of a more conscious and explicit process first of mentorship, and next of collaboration.

The findings also suggest ways in which what we know about poetry might be translated to other domains of human activity. Our concern was only with the field of poetry, and with the making of highly successful poets. But the role of parents and grandparents, primary and secondary school teachers, and community networks, is clearly of vital importance in switching on and sustaining high level poetic practice. So too, parents who model and transfer knowledge about particular skills and processes – from carpentry to neuroscience – can expose small children to the complexities and fascinations of what must seem arcane human endeavours. Teachers who not only focus on curriculum content, but are also capable of exposing their young students to a variety of activities and skills, and who are alert to the ways in which various children respond to various triggers, are likely to function as important intermediaries in allowing those children to find the practices where they might flourish. And both secondary and tertiary teachers who are sufficiently observant to notice when their students have been switched on, galvanised, captivated by a subject area or practice, and who can facilitate not just their exposure to such practices, but also the validation of their early efforts, are well placed to help the next generation of practitioners, in any field, find their own path to creative excellence.

Acknowledgements

This research was supported under the Australian Research Council's Discovery Projects funding scheme, project number DP130100402. We thank our co-investigators, Professors Michael Biggs and Kevin Brophy, and Associate Professor Paul Magee, and acknowledge the enormous support in the initial stages of the project provided by the late Dr Sandra Burr. Our thanks too to the many poets who generously contributed their knowledge and experience to this project.

Sources

Asimov, Isaac 2014 'On creativity', *MIT Technology Review* (20 October), http://www.technologyreview.com/view/531911/isaac-asimov-asks-how-do-people-get-new-ideas/?utm_source=digg&utm_medium=email, accessed 25 November 2015

Auden, WH 1995 'Phantasy and reality in poetry', in Bucknell, Katherine and Nicholas Jenkins (eds), *'In Solitude, for Company': W.H. Auden After 1940, Unpublished Prose and Recent Criticism*, Oxford: Clarendon Press, 177–96

Australia Council for the Arts 2015 *Arts Nation: an overview of Australian arts,* Sydney: Australia Council

Barthes, Roland 1979 'Lecture in Inauguration of the Chair of Literary Semiology, Collège de France, January 7, 1977' (trans by Richard Howard), *October* 8 (Spring): 3–16

Bourdieu, Pierre 2010 *Sociology is a martial art: Political writings by Pierre Bourdieu* (trans PP Ferguson, R Nice & L Wacquant), New York: The New Press

Brand, P. Z. 2015 'The Role of Luck in Originality and Creativity', *The Journal of Aesthetics and Art Criticism*, 73.1: 31–55

Cobb, Elizabeth 1977 [1959] *The Ecology of Imagination in Childhood*, New York: Columbia University Press

Collins, Randall 1987 'A Micro-Macro Theory of Intellectual Creativity: The Case of German Idealist Philosophy', *Sociological Theory* 5.1: 47–69

Collins, Randall 1989 *The Sociology of Philosophies: A global theory of intellectual change*, Cambridge MA: Harvard University Press

Cowper, William 1835 'Retirement', in *The Poems of William Cowper, Esq. of the Inner Temple*, Complete in One Volume, New York: Charles Wells, 143–64

Damon, Maria and Ira Livingston (eds) 2009 'Introduction', in *Poetry and Cultural Studies: A Reader* (Urbana and Chicago: University of Illinois Press, 1–17

Deleuze, Gilles and Felix Guattari 1986 *Kafka: Toward a minor literature* (trans Dana Polan and Réda Bensmaïa), Minneapolis: University of Minnesota Press

Deleuze, Gilles and Félix Guattari 1987 *A Thousand Plateaus: Capitalism and schizophrenia* (trans Brian Massumi), Minneapolis & London: University of Minnesota Press

Derrida, Jacques 1987 *The Truth in Painting* (trans by Geoff Bennington and Ian McLeod), Chicago: University of Chicago Press

DuPlessis, Rachel Blau 2012 'Social Texts and Poetic Texts: Poetry and Cultural Studies', in Cary Nelson (ed), *The Oxford Handbook of Modern and Contemporary American Poetry*, Oxford and New York: Oxford University Press, 53–70

Fischer, Gerhard, Elisa Giaccardi, Hal Eden, Masanori Sugimoto and Yunwen Ye 2005, 'Beyond binary choices: Integrating individual and social creativity', *International Journal of Human-Computer Studies* 63.4-5: 482–512

Fletcher, Robert 1893 'The Poet – is he born, not made?', *American Anthropological Association* 6.2 (April): 117–36

Foucault, Michel 1973 *The Order of Things: An Archaeology of the Human Sciences*, New York: Vintage Books

Foucault, Michel 1986 'Of Other Spaces' (trans by Jay Miskowiec), *Diacritics* 16.1 (Spring): 22–27

Gaut, Berys 2010 'The Philosophy of Creativity' *Philosophy Compass* 5.12: 1034–46

Glaveanu, Vlad Petre 2011 'Creativity as Cultural Participation', *Journal for the Theory of Social Behaviour* 41.1: 48–6

Kerouac, Jack 1995 *The Portable Jack Kerouac* (ed. Ann Charters), New York: Penguin

Lingis, Alphonso 1994 *The Community of Those Who Have Nothing in Common*, Bloomington and Indianapolis: Indiana University Press

Mondak, Jeffery J 2010 *Personality and the Foundations of Political Behavior*, Cambridge: Cambridge University Press

Müller-Funk, Wolfgang 2012 *The Architecture of Modern Culture: Towards a Narrative Cultural Theory*, Berlin and Boston: Walter de Gruyter GmbH

Nochlin, Linda 1988 *Women, Art, and Power and Other Essays*, New York: Harper and Row

Nussbaum, Martha 2001 *Upheavals of Thought: the Intelligence of Emotions*, Cambridge: Cambridge University Press

O'Sullivan, Simon 2005 'Notes Towards a Minor Art Practice', *Drain: Journal of Contemporary Art and Culture* 2.2 (October), http://drainmag.com/index_nov.htm

O'Sullivan, Simon 2012 'From Stuttering and Stammering to the Diagram: Towards a Minor Art Practice?', in Mieke Bleyen (ed), *Minor Photography: Connecting Deleuze and Guattari to Photography Theory*, Leuven: Leuven University Press, 3–16

Oliver, Mary 1994 *A Poetry Handbook*, San Diego: Harcourt Brace & Co

Rich, Adrienne 1973 'Song', in *Diving into the wreck: Poems 1971-1972*, New York: WW Norton & Co

Ringler, William 1941 'Poeta Nascitur Non Fit: Some Notes on the History of an Aphorism', *Journal of the History of Ideas* 2.4 (October): 497–504

Sefton-Green, Julian 2000 'From creativity to cultural production: shared perspectives', in Julian Sefton-Green and Rebecca Sinker (eds), *Evaluating creativity: making and learning by young people*, London: Routledge, 215–230

Shamsie, Kamila 2015 'Let's have a year of publishing only women', *The Guardian* (5 June), https://www.theguardian.com/books/2015/jun/05/

kamila-shamsie-2018-year-publishing-women-no-new-books-men

Sommerer, Christa and Laurent Mignonneau 2015 'Living Poetry', *Artificial Life* 21.3: 313–319

Storr, Anthony 1989 *Solitude: A return to the self*, New York: Ballantine Books

Throsby, David, Jan Zwar and Callum Morgan 2018 *Australian Book Publishers in the Global Industry: Survey method and results*, Research paper 1/2018 (February), Sydney: Macquarie University

Weinberg DB, and A Kapelner 2018 'Comparing gender discrimination and inequality in indie and traditional publishing', *PLoS ONE* 13.4; https://doi.org/10.1371/journal

Williams, William Carlos 1966 'Danse Russe', in *The William Carlos Williams Reader*, ed ML Rosenthal, New York: New Directions

Wood, Charlotte 2016 *The Writing Room*, Sydney: Allen and Unwin

Zwar, Jan, David Throsby, Thomas Longden 2015 *Australian authors* Industry Brief No. 3: Authors' Income. The Australian book industry: Authors, publishers and readers in a time of change (October), Sydney: Macquarie University